"A really short book, sl
only historically true
What more could you v

**PETER WILLIAMS,**

*We Trust the Gospels?*

"Christianity stands or falls on the truth of the resurrection, and this is the pithiest, zestiest case for the resurrection that I've seen. Whether you are looking to renew your faith or exploring the evidence for the first time, McLaughlin will guide you along the way—in roughly the time it takes to find all the Easter eggs."

**MOLLY WORTHEN,** Associate Professor of History, The University of North Carolina at Chapel Hill

"This compact book explains in a simple but profound way the reasons for believing in the resurrection of Jesus and of the Christian."

**IAN HUTCHINSON,** Professor of Nuclear Science and Engineering, Massachusetts Institute of Technology; Author, *Can a Scientist Believe in Miracles? An MIT Professor Answers Questions on God and Science*

"Rebecca McLaughlin reveals that the story of Jesus is both believable and beautiful, especially for those searching for hope, for Easter is much more than a holiday filled with egg hunts and chocolate bunnies. If this Jesus of Nazareth really did live a sinless life, die a substitutionary death, and then come back to resurrection life, everything changes; because it means you can be fully known, yet fully loved, by the Creator God of the universe, who gives us more than holidays—for he gives us himself, forever."

**JULIUS J. KIM, PHD,** President, The Gospel Coalition

REBECCA McLAUGHLIN

# IS EASTER

---

# UNBELIEVABLE?

thegoodbook.com | thegoodbook.co.uk
thegoodbook.com.au | thegoodbook.co.nz | thegoodbook.co.in

ISBN: 9781784988302 | Printed in the UK

Design by Drew McCall

# Contents

*For Katherine,*
*with hope that God is making himself obvious*

# Introduction

"**M**ummy, what do mermaids eat?" This question came from my three-year-old, Luke. "Mermaids aren't real," I explained. He followed up: "Are elephants real?"

He's subsequently wondered about snakes, cows, pigs, and monkeys—despite having seen some of these in the flesh! I guess it's confusing when you're three. I read him stories about both real and imaginary things, so how is he to know the difference? One solution would be for me to just read him works of fact. But so many of the best stories feature not-quite-real things: magic, mermaids, dragons, and implausibly happy endings. Perhaps that's why, as I was idly scrolling Instagram the other day, this block quote hit me like a cobra's strike:

> "*Reading stories is a gentle way for a child to encounter the hardest truth that shadows mortal life: There are no happy endings.*"[1]

It was from an essay in the *New York Times* by author Margaret Renkl. My first, instinctive, gut reaction was to shout out, "That's not true!"

It was a predictably human response. Religious or not, we're primed to believe in happy endings. We want (as one agnostic friend of mine once said) "the universe to have a plan for us"—and a purpose beyond the plan of using our remains as fertilizer. But is it all just wishful thinking?

In car rides with my kids right now, we're listening to Peter Pan. Famously, when the fairy Tinkerbell is dying, she tells Peter she thinks she could get well again if children believed in fairies. Peter appeals to children everywhere, "If you believe ... clap your hands; don't let Tink die."[2] However old we might be, part of us will want to clap when this appeal comes—if not for fairies, then for something magical to lift us out of the mundane and neverlasting.

So, are these happy endings just a scam—a gentle lie we tell to kids until they're old enough to know the truth? Or might there truly be a way for us to live (as fairy tales put it) "happily ever after"?

In this short book, I want to make a hope-filled case that the answer to that last question is "Yes." I want to look at the outrageous claim that, almost two millennia ago, a man who had died an unbelievably horrible death came back to unbelievably wonderful life—and offers to include us in this life, if we will trust in him.

The resurrection of the 1st-century Jewish rabbi known as Jesus of Nazareth is something Christians celebrate each Sunday, but especially at Easter. If you're hazy on the details of the story, never fear: we'll do a recap on the life, death, and apparent resurrection of Jesus in chapter 1. But rather than just retelling the story in this book, I want to explore whether it might actually be true. To do this, we will ask hard questions about Easter. Not "Is there an Easter Bunny?" or "How many chocolate eggs can I legitimately eat?" But questions that snip through the frills that have accrued around the Easter holiday and that cut to its 1st-century heart.

To start with, Christians claim that Jesus was a real person who lived and died in history. So, in chapter 1, we'll ask, "Is Jesus' life historical?" Second, Christians believe that Jesus' death wasn't just an example of Roman brutality but that he'd planned to die as a substitute for sinners, to take the punishment we all deserve for turning against God. This raises moral questions about whether you and I *are* sinners, whether God is right to judge us, and whether one person being punished on behalf of others is any kind of justice. So, chapter 2 will ask, "Is Jesus' death ethical?" The logic of the cross and the hope of Christianity is tethered to the claim that Jesus physically rose from the dead, so in chapter 3, we'll ask the most Easter-ish question of all: "Is Jesus' resurrection credible?" Finally, in chapter 4, we'll question whether Jesus' offer of eternal life with him is even desirable.

I don't know how you feel about Jesus today. I don't know whether Christianity sounds to you like clothes you've long outgrown, like an outfit in which you wouldn't be seen dead, like clothing from a culture not your own, or like something you used to wear and wish you could again. I don't know whether you've been hurt by Christians or seen Christians hurting others. I don't know if you're living your best life now or trudging through a trench of hopelessness. None of us come to questions about faith without feelings: good or bad, or just indifferent. But if we're honest, we all long for hope beyond the grave—some kind of happy ending for ourselves and those we love.

Whether you think that hope of everlasting life is pure naivety or you're wondering if there might just be a God who has a plan for your life, this book is for you. I'm not going to ask you to bury your brain and clap your hands to show that you believe in fairies. Instead, I want you to ask the awkward questions, to reckon with the hardest truth that shadows mortal life, to take a fresh look at the resurrection claim, and to wonder if it is just wishful thinking or whether it might—against all odds—be all our wildest dreams come true.

You see, if Jesus really *did* come back to life, it's not just a matter of magical curiosity, like "What do mermaids eat?" If Jesus did come back to life, it means the Maker of all time and space has stepped into the universe for love of you. It means that you were worth his death and that he wants you in his life. It means you are more seen and known and loved than you could dare to hope and that the greatest offer ever made is sitting on the table, waiting for you to take it up. But before we look at Jesus' unbelievable offer, we need to ask, "Is Jesus' life even historical?"

# CHAPTER 1

# Is Jesus' Life Historical?

"**I**, Tiberius Claudius Drusus Nero Germanicus This-that-and-the-other (for I shall not trouble you yet with all my titles)…"

My favorite historical novel begins with these words. *I, Claudius*, by Robert Graves, is a fictionalized autobiography of a relatively little-known Roman emperor. The real Claudius was born in 10 BC and died in AD 54. He was politically sidelined for much of his life, because he was disabled. But when his nephew the emperor Caligula was killed, Claudius was the last remaining adult male in the family. So, at the age of 50, much to his surprise, Claudius became the most powerful man on earth. But unless you're something of a history nerd (or happen to have seen the 1970s TV series based on Graves's book), you may well not have heard of him.

When Claudius was a child, in an obscure part of the Roman Empire a low-income teenage girl gave birth to a son and named him Jesus. Before Claudius became emperor, the man this boy became had died upon a Roman cross. Rather than being born into the imperial family, Jesus of Nazareth was born in obscurity. He lived roughly half as long as Claudius, and he died a shameful and excruciating death. Unlike Claudius (who was an accomplished historian), Jesus never wrote a book, raised an army, or ruled a realm. And yet he has become, by any measure, the most influential person who has ever lived.

In this chapter, we'll look at the historical evidence for the basic facts of Jesus' life, and we'll ask whether the four New Testament biographies—the Gospels known as Matthew, Mark, Luke, and John—are giving us reliable testimony about this 1st-century rabbi, or whether they (like *I, Claudius*) are weaving fiction in with the facts. But first, we'll sketch the outline of Jesus' life as these Gospels tell it.

## What's the Story?

Once upon a time (in about 4 BC, to be precise), Jesus was born in Bethlehem: a small town in the southern Jewish region of Judea. The Jews were living as a subjugated racial and religious group within the Roman Empire. Jesus' mother, Mary, lived in the troubled north, in an insignificant village called Nazareth. Mary was the most common name among Jewish women of that time and place, and this Mary was sufficiently poor that the newborn Jesus was laid in an animal feeding trough. But despite her unpromising credentials, Mary claimed she'd been made pregnant by the Holy Spirit of God himself.

This claim was wild.

Unlike their pagan overlords, the Jews believed in one Creator God. This God was utterly unlike the Greek and Roman deities, who sometimes impregnated human women and spawned demigods. But Mary claimed that an angel had appeared to her and said her son would be the Son of God. What's more, the angel had said that Jesus would be God's earth-shattering, long-promised King: the Messiah (from the Hebrew) or Christ (from the Greek). Talk about great expectations!

At first, it seemed that Jesus might just be this great Messiah of the Jews. He grew to be an incredible teacher and miracle worker. People said that his words alone could stop storms, heal the sick, and even raise the dead. He claimed that he was indeed God's Son and that he was the much-anticipated Christ. But unexpectedly for such a claimant to the throne, he said he'd come "not to be served but to serve, and to give his life as a ransom for many" (Mark 10:45). In fact, as Jesus' ministry (public teaching) went on, he kept predicting not that he would *overthrow* the Romans but that he'd *die* at their hands. He said this was the plan: that he would die, so that anyone who trusts in him could live. But even his disciples didn't understand.

Then, one fateful Friday, after only a few short years of public teaching, Jesus was nailed to a Roman cross. All hope that he was God's great King was snuffed out. His disciples were devastated. His mother, Mary, and many of his other friends and followers watched Jesus die. But on the Sunday morning, another Mary from another little village named Magdala (aka Mary Magdalene) went to Jesus' tomb with some of his other female followers. These grieving women hoped to give Jesus' body the proper burial treatment. But when they came to the tomb, it was empty. Two angels showed up and explained to them that Jesus had been raised to life again. Mary Magdalene even met the risen Jesus in the flesh, and she and her companions went back to tell the other disciples what they'd seen and heard.

At first, the male disciples didn't believe the women's story. But then Jesus revealed himself to them as well. He told them that his plan had worked. Instead of defeating the Romans, he'd beaten sin and death, so anyone who put their trust in him could be forgiven by God and welcomed into everlasting life. "Thus it is written," Jesus explained, "that the Christ should suffer and on the third day rise from the dead, and that repentance for the forgiveness of sins should be proclaimed in his name to all nations, beginning from Jerusalem" (Luke 24:46-47).

That is the Easter story in a nutshell: the God of all the universe was born into poverty to die for you and me—then raised to life so we can be forgiven and live eternally beyond the grave. But is it pure naivety to think it might be true? After all, some people question whether Jesus even lived.

## Did Jesus Even Live?

If you think there's some historical doubt as to whether Jesus of Nazareth ever really walked this earth, you're not alone. One 2015 survey found that 40% of adults in the UK either didn't think that Jesus was a real, historical person or weren't sure.[3] But the evidence for Jesus' life is unmistakable. As the famously skeptical New Testament scholar Bart Ehrman puts it, "The reality is that whatever else you may think about Jesus, he certainly did exist." This view is no minority report. As Ehrman explains, it's "held by virtually every expert on the planet."[4]

You see, even if we set the Gospels aside, the basic facts of Jesus' life are attested by other early documents, written by people who didn't even like Christians. From these non-biblical documents, we know that Jesus was a 1st-century Jewish rabbi who was believed to be the Christ, crucified under the authority of the Roman governor Pilate (who ruled over Judea from AD 26/27 to 36/37), and subsequently worshiped by his followers as if he were divine.[5]

So, we know that Jesus lived. But the Gospels were written decades after Jesus' death. Can we really take their accounts of his life seriously?

## Eyewitness Testimony

I'm writing this in 2022—54 years after the assassination of civil rights activist, Rev. Dr. Martin Luther King Jr. If, instead of this book, I was writing a biography of King, I could consult with many of his close associates. If I said to them, "Of course, you can't possibly remember what Martin said to you in the days before he died," they'd look at me like I was crazy. How could they *not* remember his speeches, and the private conversations they'd had with him, and the terrible day he was murdered? These moments changed their lives, and they've been talking about their hero ever since.

Likewise, the four New Testament biographies of Jesus were all written well within the lifetimes of eyewitnesses. Mark's Gospel is generally agreed to be the first. Its author was a close associate of Simon Peter: one of Jesus' twelve official disciples. Experts believe that Mark was likely written between 35 and 45 years after Jesus' death—perhaps even earlier—and that it's mostly based on Simon Peter's memories of Jesus. In ancient historical terms, 35 to 45 years is *very* soon after someone's life to be writing their biography. For comparison, the Roman historians Suetonius and Tacitus, whose biographies tell us most of what we know about the emperor Claudius, were likely writing more than 60 years after Claudius' death.

Jesus had twelve formal disciples (also known as apostles), whose day job was to follow their rabbi and to memorize his sayings. Jesus also had many informal disciples, including many women, who traveled with him and ate up his words. After Jesus' death and resurrection, these eyewitnesses dedicated their lives to telling others about everything he'd said and done. The Gospels were all written within the lifetimes of these witnesses and record their testimony. Indeed, as New Testament scholar Richard Bauckham has shown, when the Gospel authors give us names in their narratives, they're often pointing us to the eyewitnesses whose memories they're capturing.[6] It's not like you or me being asked to remember random things we overheard decades ago. It's more like the crew that travels with U2 being asked to remember the words of Bono's early songs and the crazy things he did on the road.

John's Gospel is likely the last to have been written, some 60 years after Jesus' death. This is more like the time gap between Claudius' death and Suetonius' and Tacitus' biographies. But unlike Suetonius and Tacitus, John claims that he himself was an eyewitness of his subject's life and death, and that he even saw Jesus after his resurrection. It's not implausible that John was writing in his late seventies or early eighties about things he had witnessed in his late teens or early twenties.

So, the Gospels are close enough to Jesus—both in time and in their access to eyewitnesses—for us to see them as credible historical accounts. But how do we know that their authors weren't adding layers of fiction about Jesus to the skeleton of fact to suit their own political agenda, and that other, more authentic accounts of the life of Jesus haven't been suppressed?

## Aren't the Gospels Propaganda?

In his 2003 bestseller *The Da Vinci Code*, novelist Dan Brown popularized the idea that the real life of Jesus was suppressed by church authorities for their own political ends. The book is page-turny fiction but so far from historical fact that even my most secular grad-school historian friends were annoyed! Unlike Robert Graves in *I, Claudius*, Brown isn't painting fiction inside the lines of history but rather taking more of a splatter-paint-art approach. Specifically, he claims that the four New Testament Gospels are not our best historical sources about Jesus. But, despite his own skepticism about Jesus, scholar and best-selling author Bart Ehrman explains that the Gospels of Matthew, Mark, Luke, and John are "the oldest and best sources we have for knowing about the life of Jesus" and this is "the view of all serious historians of antiquity of every kind, from committed evangelical Christians to hardcore atheists."[7]

What's more, the idea that the Gospels are propaganda from the early church does not align well with the texts themselves. Jesus' apostles went on to be key leaders in the 1st-century church, but their portrayal in the Gospels is frankly embarrassing. Time and again, they fail to believe what Jesus says. Jesus even calls them "you of little faith" (Matthew 8:26). Peter gets especially bad press. For instance, when Jesus first predicts his death, Peter tries to talk him out of it. Jesus responds, "Get behind me, Satan!" (Mark 8:33). Later, Peter swears he's ready to die with Jesus. But Jesus tells him that instead, that very night, Peter is going to deny even knowing Jesus three times—and Jesus is right (Mark 14:26-31; 66-72)! If anyone had power in the early church to censor the stories about Jesus, it was Peter. Yet even Mark's Gospel (the one that's based on Peter's own testimony) paints Peter in a very shameful light.

On top of this, as we'll see later, the role that women play in all the Gospels cuts against the culture of that day. In particular, all four Gospels present women as the key eyewitnesses of Jesus' resurrection at a time when the testimony of women would not have been seen as credible. If the Gospel authors *had* been making things up to serve the political agenda of the early church, they did an extremely poor job!

So, the Gospels were written early, were based on eyewitness accounts, are recognized by experts as the best historical sources we have for the life of Jesus, and seem to have been constrained by the truth even to the extent of exposing the faults of the most influential Christian leaders of their day.

But while he thinks the Gospels are the best historical sources about Jesus that we have, Ehrman argues that if we read the Gospels side by side and notice the differences between them, we'll find they aren't as trustworthy as Christians imagine. So, is this true?

## Do the Gospels Contradict Each Other?

My weekly Bible-study group right now is doing a "two-minute testimony" series, where different members of the group share how they came to trust in Jesus. We don't set a timer, and people usually talk for longer. But even so, they're offering a massively condensed description of their life. If we redid the series after everyone had shared and took recordings of the testimonies, my guess is that each person would tell their story in a slightly different way the second time.

The Gospels are condensed biographies, cramming years of Jesus' words and actions into books that can be read in 1.5 to 2.5 hours. John ends his Gospel like this: "Now there are also many other things that Jesus did. Were every one of them to be written, I suppose that the world itself could not contain the books that would be written" (John 21:25). So, we know that the Gospel authors were being extremely selective, both in the stories they told and in the parts of each story that they highlighted. This is one reason why two different Gospels sometimes capture different pieces of the same story.

The Gospel authors aren't just dry historians. They're storytellers, squeezing every ounce of meaning out of every page. Sometimes, instead of ordering their stories chronologically, they put two stories next to each other to make a point. Sometimes, they focus on one person in a story. For instance, Mark's Gospel tells us that on his way out of Jericho, Jesus healed a blind beggar named Bartimaeus (Mark 10:46-52), while Matthew tells us that Jesus healed two anonymous blind beggars in that place (Matthew 20:29-34). These seem at first like contradictory accounts. But the Gospel authors often choose to highlight one individual in a story, and, if you think about it, we do the same. For instance, I just had a conversation with my friend Julie. I might tell my husband, Bryan, about it later. If I do, I'll likely leave out the fact that Grace was also in the room, as Bryan doesn't know Grace and she was incidental to the conversation. The people healed by Jesus in the Gospels are almost always left anonymous. But Mark chooses here to focus on Bartimaeus and to tell us his name because this blind man became an eyewitness of Jesus, and may even have been known to some of Mark's readers.

As we compare Gospel accounts, we also need to bear in mind that the Gospels were originally written in Greek, which was the international language of the Roman Empire. But Jews of Jesus' time and place spoke Aramaic as their first language. So, at least some of the time, the Gospel authors would have been translating Aramaic into Greek. It's similar in my Bible-study group, where multiple members speak English as their second language. When my friend Jorge, who comes from

Peru, shared his two-minute testimony, he was not only summarizing what happened; he was also, at times, translating from Spanish to English. The fact that the Gospels were written in Greek, while Jesus likely taught in Aramaic, doesn't mean their stories about Jesus are untrustworthy, any more than Jorge's account of his faith journey is suddenly untrustworthy because he was translating into the shared language of the group. But it's one reason why we sometimes see things Jesus said recorded in somewhat different words in one Gospel versus another. We also need to recognize that Jesus would have given similar teachings in different places as he traveled around. There were no YouTube videos to propagate his message!

So, when it comes to the Gospels, we shouldn't imagine them as four different witnesses in a courtroom, summoned independently to give an account of what happened on the day of the crime. We should think of them more like four eulogies at a funeral, delivered from different perspectives but building on each other. Very likely, Matthew and Luke had access to all or part of Mark's Gospel when they wrote their own significantly longer biographies of Jesus. John may well have known Mark's Gospel too. These authors added testimony from their own eyewitness sources and told stories in their own way.

In summary, the Gospels were not written long after the events they record by people who had no access to what Jesus really said and did. They were written well within the lifetimes of the men and women who went everywhere with Jesus, and they offer us condensed biographies of a man who healed hundreds of sick people and preached hundreds of sermons in dozens of towns and villages. By any reasonable historical measure, the Gospels have very good credentials— much better, in fact, than many documents we take to be reliable guides when it comes to the lives of other ancient figures.

The book, *I, Claudius*, blends historical fact with fictional speculation about the life of this unlikely emperor. But there's good reason to believe that Matthew, Mark, Luke, and John do not enhance fact with fiction. Rather, they give us real access to eyewitness testimony about Jesus of Nazareth. If they had felt free to make things up, they would not have invented the failure of the male disciples or the prominent role played by the female disciples— especially as witnesses of Jesus' crucifixion, burial, and resurrection. So, what should we make of this most famous death in all of history? That's the question for our next chapter.

# CHAPTER 2

# Is Jesus' Death Ethical?

The 2021 James Bond movie *No Time to Die* begins with a young girl and her mother in an isolated house. The mother is a mess, sprawled on the couch. The daughter, Madeleine, sees a creepy, masked man's face at the window. The man enters the house and shoots her mother dead before pursuing Madeleine across a frozen lake. It's terrifying.

Bond films tend to *end* with Bond having drinks with a pretty girl on a tropical island. But in this film, that scene happens right after the opening chase, as we see the grown-up Madeleine and Bond at a beach. Then, rather than ending with Bond having drinks, the movie ends with Bond's colleagues raising a glass to his memory and a new agent 007 taking his place.

My best friend and her husband saw this film when it came out, and she told me the spoiler. (Apologies if I've just done the same for you!) I knew from the first that

Bond would die. But I didn't know why. I had to see the movie to discover that.

If you know anything about Jesus, you'll know that he died on a cross. But to get a better sense of *why* he died, we need to mine the Gospels and hear their spoilers about his much-anticipated death. In this chapter, we'll see how Jesus both predicted and explained his death, and we'll ask whether his analysis of what would happen at the cross makes moral sense. The Friday before Easter, when Christians strangely celebrate the death of their leader, is often called "Good Friday." In this chapter, we'll see why the cross—which may at first appear *unjust*—is ultimately very good.

## The Hero's Death

Bond's death is fittingly heroic. The film's extremely creepy villain, Lyutsifer Safin (who murdered Madeleine's mother in the opening scene), has been developing a large-scale biological weapon. But before he can unleash it on the world, Bond finds Safin's factory on a remote island. He rescues Madeleine and their five-year-old daughter, Mathilde, whom Safin has abducted. Then Bond kills Safin. His work complete, Bond tells the British navy to send a missile to destroy the factory. But at the last minute, Bond finds he has to go back in. Knowing he'll die when the missile hits, he spends his final moments talking to Madeleine via radio. Bond had hoped to restart his life with the woman he loves. Instead, he dies knowing that he's saved Madeleine, their daughter, and the world. He did not plan to die. But it was worth it.

Like the screenwriters of *No Time to Die*, the Gospel authors offer us their hero as the Savior of the world. But Matthew, Mark, Luke, and John present Jesus' death not as a tragic by-product of his mission but rather as its central goal. After the third time that he predicts his death, Jesus gives his disciples this topsy-turvy leadership principle: "Whoever would be great among you must be your servant, and whoever would be first among you must be slave of all." Then he explains his rationale:

> For even the Son of Man came not to be served but
> to serve, and to give his life as a ransom for many.
> (Mark 10:43-45)

"The Son of Man" was Jesus' favorite way of referring to himself. It channeled an Old Testament prophecy, written several hundred years before, about one "like a son of man" coming on the clouds of heaven and receiving an everlasting, universal kingdom from God himself (Daniel 7:13-14). But Jesus explained that his great mission as the universal, everlasting King was not to lord it over others but to die so that they could live. Indeed, the Gospels depict Jesus as the perfect Son of God, who came to die an agonizing death for *other people's* sin. This is a stunning story. But it raises three legitimate concerns. First, what kind of God would punish people for their sin? Second, who qualifies as a sinner? Third, how is the brutal killing of an innocent man in the place of sinful people *just*? We'll look at each of those questions in turn.

## What Kind of God Would Punish Sin?

I'm writing this a few days after 19 children and two teachers were gunned down in an elementary school in Uvalde, Texas. As the mother of three young kids, I can hardly imagine what the parents of all those murdered little ones are feeling. Their anger and their helpless grief must be unbearable. I'm moved to tears by even thinking about what they're going through and what their children went through on that awful day, as they awaited help and no help came. We rightly mourn their little lives. We also know they weren't the only children murdered or abused around the world that day—and every day. Most of these heartbreaking events will never make the headlines. How are we to begin to make sense of them?

We can ascribe some portion of horrific acts to mental illness. We can observe the ways in which a person's background can affect how he or she relates to others, even to the point of murdering children. We can explain how ideologies of various kinds can stimulate atrocities and chart how, for example, Naziism turned well-educated, modern people into genocidal killers. But if we took a survey of the crimes committed right across the world today, we'd also have to recognize the rawness of the evil. We may not use the language of *sin*, but all of us must find a way to talk about the human capacity for wrong. We may see its ravages up close or only in the headlines. But one thing all human cultures have in common across time and place is the spilling of seemingly innocent blood. When evils like the shooting in Uvalde come into view, we might stop wondering, "What kind of God would punish people for their sin?" and ask instead, "Where is the God of justice, and why doesn't he step in?" The answer that the Gospels give us to this question is twofold: he has, and he will.

## The God Who Steps In

The Gospels claim that the 1st-century Jew known as Jesus of Nazareth is the Creator God of all the universe in human form. From Mary's first encounter with the angel who said her son would be the Son of God (Luke 1:26-38) to Jesus' own claim to be one with the one true God (John 10:30), the Gospels tell us that if we look at Jesus, we'll see God himself (John 14:8-9). Because of this, they also claim that Jesus is the rightful judge of all the earth. He is the God who made us, so our hearts and lives belong to him. Just as he wrote the laws of gravity, he has also written the laws of right and wrong. But rather than setting the dividing line of good and evil with us firmly on the side of good, Jesus' standards seem to rule us out.

"You have heard that it was said to those of old, 'You shall not murder; and whoever murders will be liable to judgement,'" Jesus explains. "But I say to you that everyone who is angry with his brother will be liable to judgment" (Matthew 5:21-22). I may think I'm completely different from the shooter in Uvalde. But according to Jesus' standards, I've committed murder too. He goes on, "You have heard that it was said, 'You shall not commit adultery.' But I say to you that everyone who looks at a woman with lustful intent has already committed adultery with her in his heart" (Matthew 5:27-28). Once more, I may think that I'm not the kind of person who would cheat on their husband or wife. But Jesus says I am.

When Jesus is asked which is the greatest commandment in the law, he replies:

> *"You shall love the Lord your God with all*
> *your heart and with all your soul and with*
> *all your mind. This is the great and first*
> *commandment. And a second is like it: You shall*
> *love your neighbor as yourself."*
>
> *(Matthew 22:36, 37-39)*

If I am honest, I have failed at both. And it's not just that I missed some minor detail of God's moral law. I've screwed up on the most important ones of all: to love

God with everything I have, and to love those around me as myself.

When Jesus is asked a follow-up—"Who is my neighbor?"—things get worse. He doesn't say, *Oh, your neighbor means your family and friends—the people in your demographic who live on your street*. Instead, he answers with a story about someone showing sacrificial love to a stranger from the racial and religious group which they had been raised to *hate* (Luke 10:25-37). In other words, your neighbors are not just your friends but also your enemies. What's more, Jesus also tells a terrifying story about a rich man who goes straight to hell apparently for failing to care for the poor man who lived on his doorstep (Luke 16:19-31). You and I may not have people literally starving on our doorstep. But very likely we have money we could give to help the starving in the world today, and instead we hoard that money for ourselves and give (at best) a small proportion of our income to the poor.

From Jesus' perspective, we are utter moral failures. We don't need a self-improvement plan; we need a Savior.

## Are We Really Sinners?

You may be thinking, "Listen, I know I'm not perfect, but I'm basically a good person. How can you possibly say that I'm no different from a murderer?" If that's your gut reaction, let me invite you to do a secret experiment on yourself. It's one I sometimes do myself.

Look at the time right now (for me, it's 10:47 a.m.). Between now and this time tomorrow, imagine you have a bubble over your head from which everyone can read your thoughts.

If I knew that was true of me, I'd cancel all my plans and hole up in my room. It's not that *all* my thoughts are bad. But, if I'm honest, anyone who saw my thoughts for even just one day would run from me.

You might say, "Fine, but neither of us have committed murder." No. But is this really because we're cut from different cloth than any murderer, or more because we've been dealt a different hand? *No Time to Die* begins with Safin murdering Madeleine's mother. But as the film unfolds, we find that that murder was revenge; his family was killed when he was a kid, and it was Madeleine's father's doing. To some extent, we understand. Perhaps, with Safin's horrific background, we'd have done what he did. We might conclude that murderers—like the fictional Safin, or the too terribly real 18-year-old who murdered all those children in Uvalde—don't truly deserve God's judgment after all. But Jesus' conclusion is the opposite: they *do* deserve God's judgment, and so do we. And yet, instead of crushing us, Jesus came to be crushed *for* us.

You see, at the same time as Jesus puts us in the Safin-sinful camp, he also groups us with Madeleine. Like Safin, we deserve to die. Like Madeleine, we are loved. Jesus loves us so much that he was glad to die *for* us. This is the scandal of the Gospels. Jesus didn't come for righteous people but for sinners who will put their trust in him.

That brings us to our third legitimate concern. Suppose for a moment this is true. Suppose you and I deserve God's judgment for our sin. Suppose Jesus really *did* step in for love of us and take our punishment. Then how is the death of an innocent man in the place of guilty people *just*?

## How Is the Cross Just?

When Bryan and I married in 2007, we moved in together and merged our bank accounts. This was a very good deal for me. I had some student debt, and he had assets from running a landscaping business through his teenage years. So, when our bank accounts were combined, he took my debt, and I took his cash. (Now that I put it that way, it sounds bad—but I promise I didn't marry him for his small savings!) Our wedding vows included this pledge: "All that I am I give to you, and all that I have I share with you." This is a very scary vow to make. But it springs out of the biblical idea that when two people marry, they become "one flesh" (Genesis 2:24).

According to the Bible, when someone puts their trust in Jesus, they get spiritually joined to him more deeply than a husband and a wife are joined in marriage. Two become one. So, as when my husband's money canceled out my student debt, when Jesus died upon the cross, he carried all the sin of those who put their trust in him. What's more, he gave them all his goodness. Jesus is not a random bystander hauled in to pay for other people's sin. He is, as Matthew's Gospel puts it, "God *with* us" (Matthew 1:23). He freely took our sin upon himself so that we are free to live eternally with him. Why? Because of love.

## Love Dies

If you read the New Testament Gospels, you'll find that the love revealed in Jesus' life was unbelievable. He fed the hungry, welcomed outcasts, healed lepers, defended women, broke through racial and cultural barriers, stood up to bullies, and gathered little children in his arms. What's more, if you look into the history of ethics, you'll find that our most basic moral beliefs today (for example, our belief that human beings are all fundamentally equal, regardless of race or sex or nationality or socioeconomic status) have ultimately come to us from the life and teachings of Jesus—whether we realize it or not.[8] But the love shown in Jesus' death is even more stunning than the love shown in his life.

"This is my commandment," Jesus declared to his disciples on the night he was arrested, "that you love one another as I have loved you. Greater love has no one than this, that someone lay down his life for his friends" (John 15:12). He said these words fully knowing that his so-called friends would all abandon him that night.

He said it knowing that he was heading for the cross: an instrument of torture so horrific that it was not even spoken of in polite Roman society. He said it knowing that the cross had always been the plan.

We've sanitized the cross through two millennia of beatific art. But its reality was unimaginably cruel. Its victims hung for hours being gradually asphyxiated, while people gazed upon their naked, beaten, and humiliated bodies. The Romans saw it as a fitting death for slaves who had rebelled against the power of Rome. But the physical pain of crucifixion was only part of Jesus' suffering. According to the Gospels, Jesus also faced the spiritual pain of God's just judgment on our sin. Shortly before he was arrested, Jesus pleaded, "Father, if you are willing, remove this cup from me. Nevertheless, not my will, but yours, be done" (Luke 22:42). The cup in question was the cup of God's wrath: a powerful Old Testament metaphor for God's judgment on whole nations for their sin.

So, do the Gospels show us Jesus as the unwilling victim of his heavenly Father's anger? No. They show us his deep, human dread of what he chose to face. But also, they show how completely in control he was—predicting time and again that he would die. What's more, they show us Jesus warning of the stark reality of hell and how he would himself one day come back to earth as judge. We may not think that sin requires punishment. Our deep, cultural belief that human beings are by nature good, and that bad things only happen as a consequence of faulty education or childhood trauma, makes the idea that God is right to judge us alien to our way of thinking. But Jesus takes a very different view. He claims that evil comes out of our very hearts (Mark 7:20-23) and that God is absolutely right to judge us for our sin.

What's more, when Jesus hung upon the cross, he didn't just absorb his *Father's* righteous anger against sin. He also took his *own*. Just as Bond summoned the missile to destroy the evil factory and then stood on its roof awaiting the blast, so Jesus called down judgment on our sin and then stood in our place and suffered its blast. As the one who is God in human flesh, Jesus chose to die so we could be forgiven and embraced by God himself—because of love.

In *No Time to Die*, Bond dies as savior of the world, and of the woman and child he loves. When Jesus died as the real Savior of the world, he had more love in his heart for you than Bond could ever feel for Madeleine. He is the rightful judge and King of all the earth. But he loves us so much that he came not to be served, but to serve, and to give his life up for our sake.

# CHAPTER 3

# Is Jesus' Resurrection Credible?

A week before Easter in 2016, I emailed a professor friend of mine named Ian Hutchinson and asked, "Can you write an article on why you believe that Jesus rose from the dead?" At the time, my job included helping Christian professors at world-class universities write and speak about their faith. Hutchinson is a professor of Nuclear Science and Engineering at the Massachusetts Institute of Technology (MIT). He's authored more articles on plasma physics and nuclear fusion than you and I have had hot breakfasts. But in his article "Can a scientist believe in the resurrection? Three hypotheses," he argued for something he's even more committed to than physics: his belief that on the third day after he was crucified, Jesus of Nazareth physically rose from the dead.

For many today, the resurrection claim is dead on arrival. Unlike our gullible 1st-century forebears, we modern scientific folk can't possibly believe in miracles like that! But Hutchinson explains that science cannot disprove the resurrection because miracles aren't something that science is equipped to address. "Natural science describes the normal reproducible working of the world of nature," he explains. "Miracles like the resurrection are inherently abnormal."[9] What's more, the common assumption that science offers us an alternative hypothesis to faith in God is quite misleading. As Hutchinson points out, the people who first developed what we now call science, in the 16th and 17th centuries, did so precisely *because* they believed that the universe had a rational Creator, whose blueprint for creation might be discerned by human beings made (as the Bible claims) in God's own image.[10]

So, if science can't help us discern whether or not Jesus rose from the dead, what kind of evidence *should* we consider? "Contrary to increasingly popular opinion," Hutchinson explains, "science is not our only means for accessing truth." He goes on: "In the case of Jesus' resurrection, we must consider the historical evidence."

In the rest of this chapter, we'll look at four pieces of historical evidence for the resurrection. My aim is not to prove beyond reasonable doubt that Jesus rose from the dead. We're too late to the historical crime scene for that. My aim is simply to show that the resurrection claim is plausible. The first piece of evidence we'll look at is the reason why we're even talking about this almost two millennia later.

## Exhibit A: The Outbreak

In AD 64—a little over 30 years after Jesus' death—the notoriously unhinged Roman emperor, Nero, blamed the Great Fire of Rome on Christians. The Roman historian Tacitus' account of the episode shares this intel about Jesus:

> *"Christus, the founder of the name, had undergone the death penalty in the reign of Tiberius, by sentence of the procurator Pontius Pilatus, and the pernicious superstition was checked for a moment, only to break out once more, not merely in Judea, the home of the disease, but in [Rome] itself, where all things horrible or shameful in the world collect and become fashionable."[11]*

As Tacitus' contemptuous description shows, Christianity was spreading fast, despite the crucifixion of its founder. In fact, it was spreading all the more after Jesus' death!

In its first few centuries, Christianity traveled in all directions. Starting in Israel, it spread not only to Europe "but also to Egypt, North Africa, and Ethiopia, to Turkey and Armenia, to Iraq, Persia, and India."[12] By AD 300, despite intense periods of persecution, historians estimate that 10% of the Roman Empire identified as Christian, and in 312, the Roman emperor himself converted.[13] The spread of Christianity has continued ever since. Today, almost one in three humans across the globe identify as followers of Jesus, making Christianity the most popular belief system in the world, and that proportion is not set to shrink but rather to grow.[14] What's more, far from Christianity being the monocultural faith of the West, followers of Jesus are far more racially and culturally diverse than followers of any other belief system, with roughly equal numbers of Christians in Europe, North America, and Africa—and a church in China growing so fast that there will be more Christians in China than in America within five years.

Of course, the extraordinary spread of Christianity, both numerically and geographically, doesn't prove that Jesus really rose again. But how a man born into a subjugated ethnic group in an obscure Roman province—who lived poor, died young, who never wrote a book, raised an army, or sat on a throne—has come to be the most impactful human in all human history does require some kind of explanation.

Crucifying troublesome popular leaders was standard practice for the Romans, and the Gospels tell us how cowardly Jesus' twelve apostles were when he was arrested. One might reasonably have expected Jesus' crucifixion to have polished off the movement. But it didn't. Instead, somehow, Jesus' little ragtag band of followers became the most successful movement-spreaders in history.

## Exhibit B: The Message

Some skeptics have suggested that Jesus of Nazareth was an inspiring rabbi who was mythologized over time, with the resurrection as the culmination of this process. The recipe is simple: take a charismatic preacher, add a virgin birth here, some miracles there, cap it all off with a resurrection and bingo: the Son of God! It sounds quite plausible at first. Indeed, the famous British skeptic Richard Dawkins imagines it this way, with "early recruits to the young religion of Christianity" being "eager to pass on stories and rumors about Jesus, without checking them for truth."[15] But Dawkins's hypothesis is untenable.

First, without the resurrection, there would have been no young religion to recruit. The Christian message is that Jesus is the Son of God, that he died to take the punishment for the sins of any who will trust in him, that he rose from the dead, and that he welcomes all who will repent and believe to live with him forevermore. It's not a story that can stop halfway. Christianity without the resurrection would be like Disney's *Frozen* without Elsa. The resurrection isn't a nice-to-have. It's fundamental to the Christian package.

Second, if the resurrection claim was the culmination of a process of mythologizing over time, with the stories about Jesus getting more and more outlandish, we'd expect the resurrection claim to crop up only in later writings about Jesus. ("I heard he healed a leper just by touching him." "Oh yeah? Well, *I* heard he could heal people from a distance, just by saying the word." "If you think that's cool, *I* heard he rose from the dead!") But the resurrection is central to the earliest Christian writings we have: letters from the apostle Paul to some of the 1st-century churches. As Paul puts it in a letter to Christians in the Greek city of Corinth, "If Christ has not been raised, then our preaching is in vain and your faith is in vain" (1 Corinthians 15:14).

Third, if Jesus' resurrection was deliberately made up, it's hard to see *how* this could have been pulled off or *why*. All of Jesus' twelve apostles (except Judas, who betrayed him and died) claimed to have seen the resurrected Jesus, so it would have taken a coordinated conspiracy to keep that story going. But many of them went on to be executed for proclaiming Jesus as the risen Lord of all. If they had knowingly fabricated Jesus' resurrection, it's wild to think they'd die for a lie!

### Exhibit C: The Romans

It might seem odd to cite the Romans who killed Jesus as evidence for his resurrection. But our knowledge of their methods helps to quash the suggestion people sometimes make: that Jesus didn't *actually* die on the cross, so what his followers witnessed was merely a resuscitation. To be sure, crucifixion was a deliberately slow-burn death. The Roman governor, Pilate, was surprised to hear that Jesus had died a mere six hours after he was crucified. But the Romans were execution experts. To finish off the criminals who were crucified on either side of Jesus, the soldiers broke their legs so they could no longer push their bodies up to gasp for breath. But Jesus was dead already. To make quite sure, they stuck a spear into his side (John 19:31-34).

You might say, "Well, you got those details from a Gospel." That's true. But we know from other historical sources that the Romans didn't mess around. If they knew anything (aside from how to take a bath), they knew how to kill. Jesus had caused quite a stir in Jerusalem. His was by far the most high-profile crucifixion that day. The idea that the soldiers botched the job and what the disciples witnessed was a resuscitation and not a resurrection is at best implausible.

## Exhibit D: The Women

Each Gospel author tells the Easter story in his own distinctive way. But they are all quite clear that Jesus' female followers were the first to find his empty tomb and hear that he had risen from the dead. Matthew and John also tell us that the women were the first to meet the resurrected Jesus in the flesh. This may not strike us as remarkable. But to 1st-century ears, it would have been.

As Bauckham explains, in the Greco-Roman world, "women were thought by educated men to be gullible in religious matters and especially prone to superstitious fantasy and excessive religious practices."[16] The 2nd-century Greek philosopher Celsus exemplified this prejudice. He laughed at the idea that a weeping woman (Mary Magdalene) was the first witness of the resurrection: "After death [Jesus] rose again and showed the marks of his punishment and how his hands had been pierced," Celsus observed, "But who saw this? A hysterical female, as you say, and perhaps some other one of those who were deluded by the same sorcery."[17] Indeed, in Luke's Gospel, we see that even Jesus' male disciples didn't believe the women (Luke 24:10-11)! If you were trying to convince 1st-century folk that something truly unbelievable had happened, the last thing that you'd do is hinge your story on the testimony of women. But that's what all four Gospel authors did.

Despite all this, Ehrman points to the women who witnessed Jesus' resurrection as evidence that the Gospel accounts *shouldn't* be seen as accurate. All four Gospels name Mary Magdalene as one of the women who went to Jesus' tomb early on the first day of the week (Sunday) and found that it was empty. But there are discrepancies between this and the other names that the Gospel authors cite. "Who was it who went to the tomb?" Ehrman asks:

> *"Was it Mary alone (John 20:1)? Mary and another Mary (Matthew 28:1)? Mary Magdalene, Mary the mother of James, and Salome (Mark 16:1)? Or women who had accompanied Jesus from Galilee to Jerusalem—possibly Mary Magdalene, Joanna, Mary the mother of James, and "other women" (Luke 24:1; see 23:55)?"*[18]

But, as Bauckham explains, the Gospel authors are not giving an exhaustive list. They're picking out particular eyewitnesses from the group to cite their sources.[19] What's more, Ehrman writes as if John claims that Mary Magdalene was alone when she saw that Jesus had risen from the dead. But actually, John makes clear that she was *not* alone. When Mary Magdalene finds Jesus' tomb empty, she reports to Peter and John, "They have taken the Lord out of the tomb, and *we* do not know where they have laid him" (John 20:2, emphasis mine).

So, if Mary Magdalene was not alone that Sunday morning, why does John focus so exclusively on her experience? Could it be that he's inviting us to stand in Mary's sandals as she weeps by Jesus' tomb? At first, when she sees Jesus, Mary doesn't recognize him. Jesus asks her, "Woman, why are you weeping? Whom are you seeking?" Thinking he's the gardener, Mary replies, "Sir, if you have carried him away, tell me where you have laid him, and I will take him away." Jesus answers her with one word: "Mary." At last, she realizes who he is. "Rabboni!" (which means "Teacher") she exclaims (John

20:15-16). This faithful female disciple has met her risen rabbi, and he sends her back to his male disciples with the message of his resurrection. "I have seen the Lord," she proclaims (John 20:18).

In his moving account of Mary Magdalene's encounter with the risen Jesus, John shows us that the resurrection is not just a curious historical event of little relevance to us today. The implications of Jesus' victory over death are unapologetically personal.

The personal impact of the resurrection is felt by millions today, including many stunningly intelligent and educated people who were not raised in Christian homes. Professor Hutchinson is one example. "I came to faith in Jesus when I was an undergraduate at Cambridge University," he recalls, "and was baptized in the chapel of King's College on my 20th birthday. The life, death, and resurrection of Jesus Christ are as compelling to me now as then." His story is one of dozens I've heard from MIT professors who are convinced Christians. Some were raised by Christian parents. Others found unlikely paths to faith—like Professor Jing Kong, who was raised an atheist in China and started following Jesus as a graduate student at Stanford University.

Many today think that our gullible, prescientific ancestors might have been easily convinced that someone rose from the dead, but that modern, educated people can't take the resurrection seriously. But I've worked with countless leading academics at universities from MIT to Cambridge, in fields ranging from physics to philosophy, and from places as diverse as England, India, China, and Iran, who *do* believe this central, historical claim of Christianity. They haven't ditched their rationality to live an anti-scientific, historically-unfounded faith. In fact, as Hutchinson observes, "The historical evidence for the resurrection is as good as for almost any event of ancient history."

But few of these professors have been drawn to Jesus by the resurrection evidence itself. Rather, they've been drawn to Jesus by his offer of life, which the resurrection makes possible. That's the offer we'll consider in our final chapter.

# CHAPTER 4

# Is Jesus' Offer Desirable?

In *Harry Potter and the Deathly Hallows*, the teenage wizard Harry hears a children's story in which three brothers are given gifts by Death. The first brother receives an unbeatable wand; the second, a resurrection stone; and the third, an invisibility cloak.

At first, he thinks the story is pure fairy tale. But as J.K. Rowling's book progresses, Harry discovers that the wand, the stone, and the cloak are real. What's more, he gets his hands on them. Far from using them to lengthen his life, however, Harry realizes that trying to evade death is a fool's errand. In fact, the person in the series who tries the hardest to escape from death is Voldemort: the evil wizard who killed Harry's parents and has tried repeatedly to murder Harry too. As Voldemort's example and that of his "Death Eater" followers ultimately show, clinging onto life at all costs is no way to live.

Our society is conflicted about death. On the one hand, we make every effort to keep ourselves away from it—not only from dying ourselves but also from encountering the reality of death at all. A doctor friend of mine told me how often she meets older patients who only really process the fact that they will die when it is imminent. On the other hand, it's become fashionable to say that it's the shortness and contingency of life that makes it meaningful. Death is not a bug in the human story. It's a feature. In the same *New York Times* essay with which this book began, Margaret Renkl quotes another author who holds this belief:

> *'No part of an embodied life is guaranteed except for death,' writes Tallu Schuyler Quinn in her new essay collection, 'What We Wish Were True'. 'To face it—however haltingly or furiously or tearfully, or on a carousel of all those swirling feelings—is to be fully alive.'*[20]

If this is true, then everlasting life, attractive as it might sound at first, is ultimately undesirable. If you and I could wave a magic wand and make all of our dreams come true, we'd start off filled with happiness. But over time, our joy would fade. Like the characters in the TV show *The Good Place*, we'd eventually find that nothing could keep us satisfied forever.

So, what do we make of Jesus' repeated claim that he can take his followers right through death and give them everlasting life with him? Is his offer even desirable?

## Like Heaven to Touch

I just picked my kids up from school, and on the way there, my streaming service played me Lauryn Hill's amazing cover of the classic song "Can't take my eyes off of you." The original was released in 1967, and it played a starring role in the classic teenage romcom *10 Things I Hate about You*, when the seemingly tough-guy hero stuns the whole school by singing it to the girl he loves while bounding down the steps of the school stadium. The line that most intrigues me is the third: "You'd be like heaven to touch." Lovers over the millennia have made this connection. Closeness with the person they're in love with feels like heaven.

What most people don't realize is that, according to the Bible, God intended it this way. Heaven, in biblical terms, is not primarily a place. Rather, heaven is the full experience of relationship with Jesus as our Savior, lover and Lord. The Bible presents human marriage at its best as a picture of Jesus' sacrificial, passionate, unfathomable love for his people (for example, Ephesians 5:25-33). It's not that the Bible authors looked at human lovers and thought, *Huh, that deep connection seems to make people happy, so let's say that Jesus' love for us is a little bit like romantic love.* No. If what the Bible says is true, God *made* us humans with an emotional capacity for intense romantic love and built it into our biology, so that the most faithful, tender, overwhelming love we can experience with another mere human would give us just a glimpse of Jesus' love for us.

Last week, I had lunch with my friend Grace, who is dying of cancer. Her husband died a decade ago, and she misses him greatly. Grace told me about a conversation she'd had with her daughter in which her daughter said she thought of heaven as the place where they'd see Papa again. Grace replied, "I think we're setting our sights too low." She loved her husband dearly, and she'd love to be with him again. But as Grace walks into the arms of death, she knows she's walking first and foremost into Jesus' arms. The best experience of love she ever felt with her beloved here on earth is like a molecule of $H_2O$ compared to the ocean of Jesus' love.

That might sound weird at first. But if we don't get this, we won't really understand what Jesus' resurrection means, what Jesus' offer is, or why we might want to say yes. Jesus is not just the means to the end of eternal life: an everlasting life dispenser. He is the person who really *is* "like heaven to touch."

But life with Jesus is no sentimental Hallmark greeting card that glosses over suffering. Instead, the love of Jesus enters into our most painful days and brings us through them into everlasting joy.

## I Am the Resurrection and the Life

In one of my favorite chapters in the Bible, Jesus is summoned by two of his close friends: Mary and Martha of Bethany. Their brother Lazarus is dying, and they send for Jesus. Their message is simple: "Lord, he whom you love is ill" (John 11:3). At first, Jesus doesn't come. He waits on purpose until Lazarus is dead.

When Jesus finally shows up, Martha comes out to meet him saying, "Lord, if you had been here, my brother would not have died. But even now I know that whatever you ask from God, God will give you." Jesus replies, "Your brother will rise again." Thinking he's talking about the Jewish belief in the resurrection of God's people on the final judgment day, Martha responds, "I know that he will rise again in the resurrection on the last day." But Jesus pulls the conversation back to here and now: "I am the resurrection and the life," he tells her. "Whoever believes in me, though he die, yet shall he live, and everyone who lives and believes in me shall never die. Do you believe this?" (John 11:21-26).

This claim is unbelievable. Jesus is declaring that he's not just someone who can bring dead people back to life—as he ultimately does for Martha's brother. He's claiming that relationship with him is what it *means* to be alive. If we are joined to him, not even death can kill us. If we are not with him, our bodies may be living for a time, but we are spiritually dead. He is the great

Creator God made man—the one who gave us life to start with—and by his death and resurrection, he can give us everlasting life beyond the grave.

Jesus made this claim again in different words on the night he was arrested. "In my Father's house are many rooms," he said to his disciples. "If it were not so, would I have told you that I go to prepare a place for you? And if I go and prepare a place for you, I will come again and will take you to myself, that where I am you may be also. And you know the way to where I am going" (John 14:2-4). One of his disciples, Thomas, asked, "Lord, we do not know where you are going. How can we know the way?" Jesus replied, "I am the way, and the truth, and the life. No one comes to the Father except through me" (John 14:5-6). Jesus is the way to be with God in heaven. But he's also God himself. Another disciple, Philip, responded, "Lord, show us the Father, and it is enough for us." But Jesus asked him, "Have I been with you so long, and you still do not know me, Philip? Whoever has seen me has seen the Father" (John 14:8-9).

If you've ever wondered if Jesus was just a good teacher who never really claimed to be God, I hope these snatches of his teaching have put that thought to rest. If Jesus isn't God made flesh, his teaching isn't good: it's unadulterated narcissism. But even as he makes these stunning claims about himself, Jesus is preparing for the cross. He is the way, the truth, and the life. But the way he brings us life is through his death.

## Two Ways

Jesus' offer is offensively exclusive. He doesn't say that he's one way to God; he says he is the *only* way by which humans can be right with God. But Jesus' claim is also utterly *inclusive* because he says that *anyone* who trusts in him can have eternal life. As Jesus hung upon the cross, one of the criminals dying next to him made this last, desperate plea: "Jesus, remember me when you come into your kingdom." Jesus replied, "Truly, I say to you, today you will be with me in paradise" (Luke 23:42-43). There was no time or opportunity for this condemned man to clean up his life. We don't know what he'd done or how he'd lived. It didn't matter. All that mattered in that moment was that he put his trust in Jesus. And instead of saying, *Well, we'll see. I'll check your score card when I have a moment*, Jesus said, *You're coming right with me*.

If heaven is primarily a place to which we might be sent—like some fabulous vacation destination in the sky—the claim that *only* those who trust in Jesus "go to heaven" seems unfair. But Jesus says he *is* the destination. Those who turn to Jesus now will find themselves with Jesus for eternity. Those who don't want Jesus now won't get him for eternity.

How bad is it to spend eternity apart from Jesus' love? It's worse than anything we could imagine. If Jesus is the things he claims to be—the source of love and life itself—not having Jesus is a fate much worse than death. My friend Grace longs to meet with Jesus after she has died. But if we haven't put our trust in Jesus as our Lord, to meet with him as judge of all the earth is a horrific prospect. "Enter by the narrow gate," Jesus warned, "For the gate is wide and the way is easy that leads to destruction, and those who enter by it are many. For the gate is narrow and the way is hard that leads to life, and those who find it are few" (Matthew 7:13-14). There is no third way, set apart for those who think they're mostly decent people who don't really need a Savior. There's only everlasting life with Jesus or eternal, soul-destroying, hope-extinguished death.

## The Last Enemy

In the last Harry Potter book, Harry visits his parents' grave for the first time, with his friend Hermione. Lily and James Potter were murdered by Voldemort when Harry was a baby. The Potters' tombstone has their names, their dates, and this quotation from the Bible: "The last enemy that shall be destroyed is death" (1 Corinthians 15:26, KJV).

> "Harry read the words slowly, as though he would have only one chance to take in their meaning, and he read the last of them aloud.
>
> "'The last enemy that shall be destroyed is death'...'
> A horrible thought came to him, and with it a kind

*of panic. 'Isn't that a Death Eater idea? Why is that there?'*

*'It doesn't mean defeating death in the way the Death Eaters mean it, Harry,' said Hermione, her voice gentle. 'It means... you know... living beyond death. Living after death.'*[21]

This Bible verse on Harry's parents' gravestone comes from the same letter by the apostle Paul that I quoted from in chapter 3. In this part of the letter, Paul is explaining that one day Jesus will destroy death forever. Paul's evidence is Jesus' own resurrection, when he showed his power over death not by evading it but by enduring it in its worst possible form—excruciating, agonizing, public execution under God's judgment for a world of sin—and coming back to life again.

The message of Easter is not that Jesus died so that we can one day float around as disembodied souls in some ethereal realm. Instead, it's that the King of all the universe has died for us, and that if we will trust in him, he'll one day bring us back to an embodied life—richer and fresher and more beautiful than anything we've felt on earth so far. If you cannot imagine everlasting life like that, I get it. Nor can I. Our frail imaginations don't have what it takes. As Paul puts it in that same letter to the Corinthian church, "What no eye has seen, nor ear heard, nor the heart of man imagined, [that is] what God has prepared for those who love him" (1 Corinthians 2:9).

This book began with Margaret Renkl's claim that "reading stories is a gentle way for a child to encounter the hardest truth that shadows mortal life: There are no happy endings." In one sense, this is true. When I read the Bible to my kids, I'm helping them to face the fact that they will one day die. But rather than explaining that their death will be the end, I'm helping them to see that it's a new beginning. The resurrection of the Son of God, who died for love of them, is proof that one day, if they trust in him, he will welcome them to everlasting life with him.

If you will put your trust in Jesus now, admit that you're a sinner who deserves God's judgment, and believe that Jesus came to take that judgment on himself—for love of you—then he will walk with you through suffering and death, and welcome you eternally to life and love with him. This is not wishful thinking, or a childlike need to clap for Tinkerbell. It is our only hope, and one to which some of the smartest people in the last 2,000 years have clung.

The title of Renkl's article is "Sadness and Loss Are Everywhere. Books Can Help." To that, I say a big "Amen." But the books that will help us the most are the Gospel accounts of Jesus' life, which give us access to his words, first spoken two millennia ago but no less relevant to us today. "I am the resurrection and the life," says Jesus, both to his disciple Martha and to you: "Whoever believes in me, though he die, yet shall he live, and everyone who lives and believes in me will never die. Do you believe this?"

## Endnotes

1.  Margaret Renkl, "Sadness and Loss are Everywhere. Books can help," *The New York Times*, April 18, 2022; https://www.nytimes.com/2022/04/18/opinion/books-death-grief-hope.html

2.  J. M. Barrie, *Peter Pan* (Canterbury Classics, 2015), p 135.

3.  https://talkingjesus.org/research-from-the-course/ (accessed August 19, 2022).

4.  Bart D. Ehrman, *Did Jesus Exist? The Historical Argument for Jesus of Nazareth* (HarperOne, 2012), p 4.

5.  For more on the evidence for Jesus' life from non-Christian sources, see Peter Williams, *Can We Trust the Gospels?* (Crossway, 2018), p 17-36.

6.  See Richard Bauckham, *Jesus and the Eyewitnesses: The Gospels as Eyewitness Testimony* (Eerdmans, 2006), p 39-66.

7.  Bart D. Ehrman, *Truth and Fiction in the Da Vinci Code* (Oxford University Press, 2004), p 102.

8.  For more on this, see secular historian Tom Holland's *Dominion: How the Christian Revolution Remade the World* (Basic Books, 2019).

9.  For more on this, see Ian Hutchinson, *Can a Scientist Believe in Miracles? An MIT Professor Answers Questions on God and Science* (InterVarsity Press, 2018).

10. For a fuller discussion of this, see "Hasn't science disproved Christianity?" in Rebecca McLaughlin's *Confronting Christianity: 12 Hard Questions for the World's Largest Religion* (Crossway: 2019), p 109-130.

11. Tacitus, Annals 15.44, quoted from Peter Williams'

excellent short book, *Can We Trust the Gospels?* (Crossway, 2018), p 20-21.

12. See Richard Bauckham, *Jesus: A Very Short Introduction* (Oxford University Press, 2011), p 1.

13. Bart Ehrman includes an appendix on the growth of Christianity pre-300 in *The Triumph of Christianity: How a Forbidden Religion Swept the World* (Simon & Schuster, 2018), p 287-294.

14. See "The Future of World Religions: Population Growth Projections, 2010-2060," https://www.pewresearch.org/religion/2015/04/02/religious-projections-2010-2050/.

15. Richard Dawkins, *Outgrowing God: A Beginner's Guide* (Random House, 2019), p 25.

16. Richard Bauckham, *Gospel Women: Studies of the Named Women in the Gospels* (Eerdmans, 2002), p 270.

17. See Richard Bauckham, *Gospel Women*, p 271, quoting Origen, "Contra Celsus", 2:55.

18. Bart Ehrman, *Jesus Interrupted: Revealing the Hidden Contradictions in the Bible (and Why We Don't Know about Them)* (HarperCollins, 2009), p 47.

19. See Richard Bauckham, *Jesus and the Eyewitnesses: The Gospels as Eyewitness Testimony* (Eerdmans, 2006).

20. Quoted in Margaret Renkl, "Sadness and Loss are Everywhere. Books can help," *The New York Times*, April 18, 2022; https://www.nytimes.com/2022/04/18/opinion/books-death-grief-hope.html.

21. J. K. Rowling, *Harry Potter and the Deathly Hallows* (Scholastic Press, 2009), p 328.

# thegoodbook
## COMPANY

Thanks for reading this book. We hope you enjoyed it, and found it helpful.

Most people want to find answers to the big questions of life: Who are we? Why are we here? How should we live? But for many valid reasons we are often unable to find the time or the right space to think positively and carefully about them.

Perhaps you have questions that you need an answer for. Perhaps you have met Christians who have seemed unsympathetic or incomprehensible. Or maybe you are someone who has grown up believing, but need help to make things a little clearer.

At The Good Book Company, we're passionate about producing materials that help people of all ages and stages understand the heart of the Christian message, which is found in the pages of the Bible.

Whoever you are, and wherever you are at when it comes to these big questions, we hope we can help. As a publisher we want to help you look at the good book that is the Bible because we're convinced that as we meet the person who stands at its heart—Jesus Christ—we find the clearest answers to our biggest questions.

Visit our website to discover the range of books, videos and other resources we produce, or visit our partner site www.christianityexplored.org for a clear explanation of who Jesus is and why he came.

Thanks again for reading,

Your friends at The Good Book Company

thegoodbook.com | thegoodbook.co.uk
thegoodbook.com.au | thegoodbook.co.nz | thegoodbook.co.in

## WWW.CHRISTIANITYEXPLORED.ORG

Our partner site is a great place to explore the Christian faith, with powerful testimonies and answers to difficult questions.